ARTHUR SOLES

Print Shops

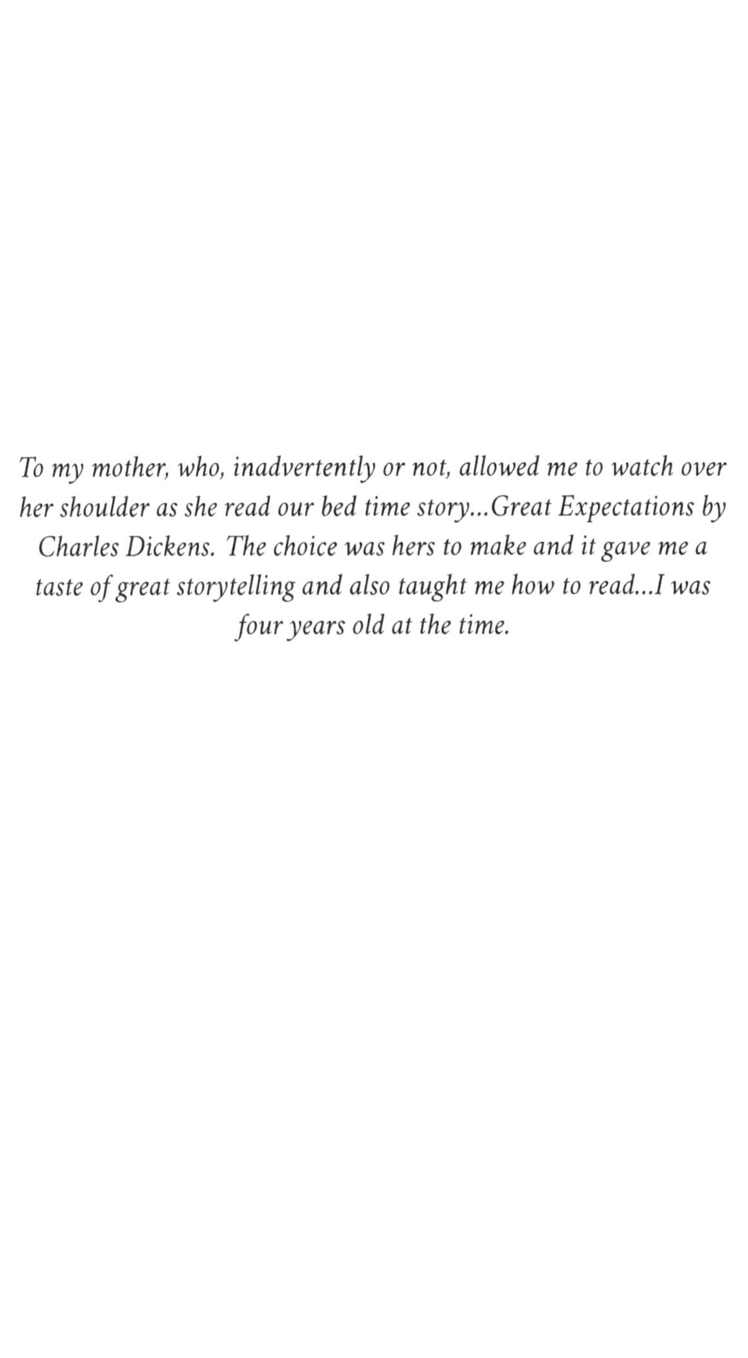

To my mother, who, inadvertently or not, allowed me to watch over her shoulder as she read our bed time story...Great Expectations by Charles Dickens. The choice was hers to make and it gave me a taste of great storytelling and also taught me how to read...I was four years old at the time.

Foreword

While this book started as a short history book, it has now evolved into more of my own story. The reason being that as I started out writing it became apparent that the story was worth more than the actual history. So be it!

Preface

I was born in 1938, the sixth of 7 children. We moved to BC from Alberta in 1943 to a quarter section on a dirt road about 20 miles out of Prince George. I lived there until I was 16 and then when the high school I was going to decided they couldn't help me with my education went out and found me a job. I was not consulted before the fact and so when I was more or less fired from school, I had a job to go to…it was of course in a Print Shop!

Acknowledgement

To my mother, who, inadvertently or not, allowed me to watch over her shoulder as she read our bed time story…Great Expectations by Charles Dickens. The choice was hers to make and it gave me a taste of great storytelling and also taught me how to read…I was four years old at the time.

To my sister-in-law who had observed that I was always writing little stories and she thought that it would be a good idea to give me something useful at Christmas time. The present was a toy printing press with lots of little letters which could be on the press and when the crank was turned I had little pages for my little newspapers. It was the greatest present I ever got!

To all the many people who worked with me over the next 65 years and were always there with help to do so many things.

1

Chapter 1

... or how I was fired from High School and ended up in a Print Shop

June 15, 1955 at 1:30 pm…the loudspeaker in the classroom rang and a gravelly voice announced "Would Arthur Soles please go to the boy's counselor office immediately." This was not a normal thing to happen, but I closed my books and walked down the hallway to the boy's counselor's office. I knocked and went inside. There I found the school principal and the counselor sitting at a desk. I announced my presence and they looked at one another and then the principal asked me to go to my locker and get everything out and then to the classroom and get everything that belonged to me and to report back to the office when I was finished.

Having done everything required I reported back to the office. The principal thanked me and asked me to accompany the

1

counselor to his car in the parking lot. He then held out his hand and shook mine and wished me the best in my future life.

I followed the counselor out to his car and he indicated I should get into the passenger side. I did as I was told and then asked the obvious question; "What is going on?" As he got into the driver's seat he asked me where I lived. I told him and we drove off. We has about and two hour drive in the country so I waited for an answer to my question.

After we left town, he looked over at me and said "This must seem very strange to you but we have decided to remove you from school at this time." He then passed me my report card for the year and a letter for my parents to read.

Fat chance of that I thought as my father was always looking for a reason to, as he would put it, "Beat me within an ounce of my life!' I guess the look on my face must have been obvious, so he carried on…"we are quite aware of the problems you face at home, so this was the only safe way to do it. When we get to your place, I will stay in the car and you will ask your mother to come and speak to me and I will explain what has happened. Your father will be having his usual afternoon nap so it should work all right.

So we drove on into the country…and with every passing mile, my apprehension mounted. So many questions…what would I do? Where would I live? My head was spinning and my heart was pounding. But eventually we pulled into the drive and he indicated that should go get my mother.

I gathered up my belongings and started up the long driveway. My mother was sitting in the back garden shelling peas and as she looked up asked why I was home at this time of day.

I told her that the man in the car wanted to speak to her and not to involve my father in any way. She got up and we walked out to the car. The counsellor got out of the car and held out and shook my mother's hand. He then proceeded to explain what was happening and why.

It seems that the school had run out of courses that I could take in Grade 12 and that the only thing they could come up with was that they could provide me a job. They had looked around and found something they thought might interest me. He went on to say that they had consulted with my oldest brother and I could stay there for a while as we figured out what to do next.

My brain was stuck on the word "job" and I couldn't imagine what I could do. So I blurted out "What kind of work did you find?"

His reply was "…in a Print Shop"

I got up with what I would need to take back with me and as I hugged my mother goodbye I told her to tell my younger brother what was happening and when it would be safe for me to come home again. She looked grimly at me and said that it will probably take a long time. I hugged her again and that was the last time I would see her for five years.

Back in the car and back into town to a little shop I had passed many times on my way uptown from school at lunch time. The counselor motioned that I should come in with him. He said hello to the man at the desk..and he pointed at the back of the room where there was a doorway. I opened the door and was immediately aware of the noise and the smell of the place. Another man was sitting at a desk and he looked round and said something about the smell and if that was offensive I could just turn around and leave. I didn't and so he told me I could start right now and I was on a monthly trial and I would get 45 cents an hour. I muttered that would be fine. As I walked into the dinn and the smell he mentioned that it was probably the first time I had ever been in a print shop.

We walked to the back of the room and he pointed at a rack of flat drawers and said, "That is a California Job Case and this is where you will be dissing the type into." I said "dissing?" and he said it is short for distributing the type after it has been in use and then the compositor would pick the letters, etc. out of the case into a type stick for use in another job.

That's how I started on the long way to be a journeyman printer!"

History of Cold Type

Explanation: Cold type refers to the setting of type which was assembled letter by letter on a stick upside down and backward. It took some time to get used to the idea but once you got on to it,,was quite easy. But in my case it was quite some time before

I ever set a line of type.

Letterpress printing is also known as relief printing. The idea is that the type set by hand letter by letter could then be locked in a chase (a metal frame) and then inked by various means such as rollers or other ways of applying a thin layer of ink on the type which then could be transferred to a sheet of paper.

By the time I arrived on the scene the presses were either large multi page presses or single sheet hand presses that the paper was inserted into a moving table that was pressed to the type in a scissor type of motion…pressing the sheet against the type and then opening again so the operator could remove the printed sheet and insert a clean sheet to be printed..so on and on.

Illustrations could be inserted along with the type so we could have pictures on our pages. So long as the frame and the type and pictures came to the height of 0.918 inches (type high) it could be used as a print in a letterpress.

The letterpress printing was developed by Johannes Gutenberg in the mid 15th century and was at the time I started much the same as it always had been. No one ever thought that it would change. You became a printer and you had a job for your lifetime.

In Canada letterpress printing was introduced in 1752 in Nova Scotia and was called the Halifax Gazette which was the first newspaper in Canada.

Further reading

Blumenthal, Joseph (1973) Art of the printed book, 1455 - 1955.
Blumenthal, Joseph (1977) The Printed Book in America.
Ryder, John (1977) "Printing for pleasure, A Practical Guide for Amateurs

2

Chapter 2

Why the big city was not such a great idea!

So returning to where I left off…I had settled down to become a good little disser…and everyone left me alone…more or less. I had become quite acquainted with the foreman and with this my horizons broadened. He would go home to Vancouver every long week and he needed a companion who could stay awake while he drove through the night, usually about 12 hours driving in his old Chevy. So I would, when we got to Vancouver, look up one of my old aunts and she would put me up for the weekend until time came for the ride home.

This went on for much of the two years until I decided that I had all the type dissing that I could handle and it seemed like a good way to go out into the wider world of printing.

The other reason that my personal life had gone from bad to worse with me moving in with my next older brother. He and his family were in the midst of becoming born again Christians and saw me as their prime target for conversion. I disagreed and even with the intervention of my sister they carried on day and night. She finally told me that getting out of town was not that bad an idea.

So on the September 1st long weekend I packed my little suitcase packed with all I owned. And we took off for the big city.

Upon arriving I checked into a small, cheap hotel in the downtown area and with a copy of the wanted ads began looking for a job. It didn't take long as I found a job advertising the need of a competent type setter. I applied in the morning and got the job. The pay wasn't great but I figured it would hold me over until something better came along.

So life at the Stamp Works started and I learned everything I would ever want to know about making rubber stamps and legal seals very quickly.

So back to the wanted ads again and this time I came up with a very interesting job. One of the larger Shops in Vancouver were looking for a stone man. This is the position in the printing industry that was the middle place between the compositors and the presses. You just had to take the forms from the typesetters and lock them in the chases for all the different types of presses. In this case there were 4 typesetters and 8 or more presses. I got the job because I was only 18 years old and not old enough to drink. Seems like all the previous stone men developed a thirst for beer early in the day which rendered them useless by noon.

The job was not that difficult and I caught on quickly. So long as the typesetters were good at their jobs and the pressmen were daily forgiving for my learning curves, all went well…and the pay was very good!

I met up with a couple of tradespeople from a small town in Saskatchewan and we got on well so we rented a nice basement suite just out of the city centre.

The winter came and went and all was well until one day I had a visit from the owner of the print shop in Prince George and he really wanted me to come back. Seems the person whom I had been apprenticed to had gone to work for the local newspaper and If I came back I would be in charge of the entire typesetting end of the business, and as a bonus they were in the process of acquiring a new typesetting machine called a Linotype which I would have to learn to use.

I was getting fairly homesick as I was not good at big city life and the winters in Vancouver could get anyone down. I talked it over with my bosses and while they wished I could stay around longer…agreed it would be a good time to leave.

So I packed up my more than one suitcase, said farewell to my roommates and caught the Rail Road to Prince George!

History of the Process

Composition (or typesetting)

The type after being assembled by the compositor or typesetter letter by letter and line by line is called typesetting. After this is done the type is then assembled into a single unit and tied off and put on a proof press where it will be proofread and any and all adjustments will be made. After this step is done then it is handed over to the stoneman where it will be locked in a chase ready for the pressmen to print it on the desired press. This process is called imposition. This can involve a single unit such as a business card or many pages as in a book.

3

Chapter 3

Back in Prince George with big changes

Getting back home was as usual. Going back to my family was out of the question so I reached out to a friend and he said he could arrange for me to rent a room on the top floor of his parent's house. I could have a hot plate and a kettle for cooking and the price would be good.

So back into the print shop again with many changes. The first one I had to master was the care and use of a Linotype. Not only would I have to use it to produce type with it I would have to know how to fix it. With over 9000 moving parts this would be a struggle.

So the owners decided the best idea was to send me back to Vancouver and they and the Linotype company would rent a warehouse floor and there I would disassemble an identical machine into all its parts and arrange them on the floor of the warehouse in such a way that I could reassemble the machine. It took a couple of weeks, but in the end I can still look at any particular part of a linotype…know what it was for and how to replace it if needed. Whew!

Two weeks later I was back in Prince George again and ready to take on the next part of my life…mechanical typesetting. We still used the hand set type for things like business cards as the Linotype only had 3 styles of printing. Small, medium and bigger type of the same typeface.

There were other machines coming out to do headlines and such but we had a very large array of various typefaces we needed and we were good at hand setting type.

It was the dawn of another decade and while things were settling down at the Print Shop more problems were appearing with the partners that owned the whole company. The stationary end of it which was run by the bookkeeping partner was being neglected by the purchase of new machinery for the printing side. Then one day he decided from the writing on the wall that the end was in sight, so he resigned and went his own way. A salesman was hired for the stationery side of it and that he would also sell printing for the printing side. But unfortunately it soon became clear that this fellow would rather go into hobby stuff rather than the more boring things like stationary.

Finally my boss came to me to announce that as the railroad north of Prince George was being completed and there was a vast area of province we could service. His idea was that I should travel north and sell printing in an area that previously had been serviced by Alberta.I was not all that keen on the idea seeing I had just got married and my daughter was on the way.

But the boss said that was fine and it would be only for a short time until we got settled in the territory and a permanent sales person could be hired for the whole region.

I said okay and found myself in the little Chevy van headed north. I soon found out that while I was a good printer and I knew our products well, I was not a salesperson. Every day was hell on wheels and I was so glad to turn around and head for home. I sold enough to show that the idea was a sound one…it just was not my thing. So I carried on for the summer.

Meanwhile things at the shop were getting really messed up without me being there at critical times and every time I came back with more orders, they were having problems getting them printed for the next train north.

Then everything came to a screaming halt when the boss was diagnosed with cancer and that he did not have long to live. He did not give up easily but in the end he died.

I was in town at the time so I called a meeting with all involved and we decided what we would do is split up the company into two pieces. I would buy the printing side and the salesperson would buy the stationery part. He brought in another partner to finance that end and I had to borrow money privately to finance the print shop.

All would have gone well except once the money was put into a bank account where the lawyers could look after it. The other fellows partner cleaned out the bank account, sold his house and moved to Australia, all in one night and was never to be heard from again.

Needless to say that was the end of the print shop and almost the end of me as well. I had a nervous breakdown and moved my family to my mothers farm outside of town and holed up there for a few months. After a while things quieted down and I had to find work again.

Work was not all that available in British Columbia so I found a job running a linotype in a newspaper in northern Alberta.

But that's another story!

Final words on it all

So I thought that I should finish it all off with a recap of what happened between 1960 and the present (2022).

Firstly I am in fact alive and well in my 83rd year and so far as I know the oldest printer in British Columbia. There are a few who would argue the case, but I count all the years working in the trade I still love as working continually in one phase or another for most of those years. I have never been unemployed longer than a couple of weeks between jobs when I was still employable. I retired 3 or 4 times only to kick the tyres and get back on the bike.

I left British Columbia in 1969 and worked for the winter in St. Paul, Alberta…not St. Albert where I thought I was going. St. Paul was the lonliest, coldest place I have ever lived and when the spring time came I looked for a nicer place to live.

I had a choice between Cardston and Hinton. I chose Hinton over Cardston because I had been through Hinton a few times and because of its close proximity to Jasper Park I thought it would suit me fine.

The man that had the little flyer there had just bought out the monthly newspaper and was in the process of setting it up. He had inherited the little multilith press and had a friend who worked in the nearby pulp mill to set it up. It was not going well and once I found that the friend who was helping him out was an engineer. Now there is nothing wrong with engineers but they always start at the end of the problem and work their way to where the problem begins. With small offset presses this is not the way to go. If you start with the present problem and fix what is causing the problem and before long it is running just fine.

So me and the press and the boss who also ran a menswear store as well with the shop in back got on just fine.

The other perk to this job was that north of Hinton was some of the best fly fishing country anywhere. So when the trout were running we would get a radio call from his friend who lived up and we would lock up paper and clothing stores and go fly fishing! What a life that was. So a couple years went by but in the second winter my daughter who was five at the time found she had problems breathing. So a quick trip to the doctor showed that she was having a problem with the high altitude and it would get worse quickly if we didn't get to lower altitude and warmer temperature.

So it was back looking again. I found a job in Osoyoos at a newspaper that needed a linotype operator and someone that could look after their little offset press that they used for flyers. Into my car again and driving through a mighty autumn snow storm between Edmonton and Calgary, I arrived in Osoyoos on October 31.

There were still some apples on the trees…I got the job and sent for the wife and kids to come on out.

The pay wasn't all that great but the food and rent were cheap so we settled down back behind the linotype and spent a lot of time lying around in the sun. The winter came and went and my daughter started in grade 1. Other than that, there was no air conditioning in the print shop as the summer became warmer and warmer. It was what you could call a hot summer. In the fall the boss installed a pretty robust air conditioner so life was pretty good that winter. But as the years went by I could see that we would be in trouble if there wasn't any more money. The boss was sympathetic and said he would do what he could do.

Then one day out of the blue the paper salesman popped in as he usually did once a month. He pulled me to the side and asked how things were going. I told him it was fabulous except for the money. He said then he had a proposition for me. It seems that the man who owned Prince George Printers at the time thought that I would fit in fine. I asked what kind of money I could expect…how would starting at $10.00 an hour with guaranteed increases every year.

I was making $2.90 an hour at the time.

So I talked it over with the editor of the paper and as there was no way he could touch that kind of money, said fine and threw us a nice going away party. I was sad to leave Osoyoos but kind of excited to be going home again.

I started at Prince George Printers and worked there for 23 years.

Over the years, the owner left most of the organization to me and he made money and I made money so all was well. Then his wife died and he decided that he didn't want to go on so he put it up for sale. He offered it to the crew but none of us were rich enough to buy it, his secretary said she could raise the money. She did and the entire crew except for me quit! I should have as well but thought I would stay on to get her on her feet. I spend the next three years teaching her everything I knew. As I was employed by the company…all my holiday benefits stayed the same. That really did not sit well with her during my annual holidays (which were 6 weeks at the time). She smiled sweetly and said go ahead. I had a wonderful holiday but as soon as go to work she called me into her office and told me that things had come to light about how I ran the company and that I was fired for incompetence and there would be no compensation!

I didn't say much but I gathered up all the evidence I had been accumulating since she took over and went straight to the labor board, explained what had happened and showed her all the little rewards etc. she kept presenting to everyone. The lady at the labor board said she would get it all sorted out…and she did.

She would only pay me the minimum severance pay and so I said OK. As I walked out the door with the check in my hand I turned and said "Didn't you forget something?" "What now? She snarled. I smiled and said "You seem to have forgotten to sign the check." "Well" said and grabbed the check and signed it.

So that was my last job in Prince George and as my marriage also came apart, there wasn't much reason to stay there.

I wandered down to Quesnel and worked for Spartan Printing for the next 9 years. I became redundant again so I retired and moved to New Westminster to go to school and learn about building web sites…moving then to Chemainus on Vancouver Island where I got involved with a newspaper man who was starting a weekly newspaper. I did his production work and also production for a native newspaper in Saskatchewan until I got shingles, shut down my little business and retired in Victoria for what I hope is the last time.

30

4

Chapter 4

Health Problems in the Print Shop.

The problems that some of the solvents such as Benzene were very dangerous to one's health. And this chemical was used extensively for cleaning the type as it evaporates very quickly. This was the odour I noticed when I first entered a Print Shop. Our hands became very soaked with this combined with the oil based inks that were used at the time. No amount of washing could ever get it out and as a result caused a great deal of problems with their hands not to mention the amount that was breathed in with the usual constant cigarette smoking.This probably is the reason that there are relatively few old printers!

This coupled with the problems once hot type became more common. The temperature of type metal (melts at 327 °C (621 °F) is alloy, consisting chiefly of lead and antimony, and sometimes small quantities of tin, copper, etc. Applied to the matrices under pressure of the pump in the casting oven. it is prone to squirt out at the operator who is only seated about 3 to 4 feet from the vise holding the type. Such squirts are caused by misalignment of the type matrices (too tight or too loose or slightly bent) and can cause a great deal of pain where it hits the skin. Most, or I would say all Linotype operators have scars from squirts.d\

The other problem equally as series is when the metal bars that feed the casing oven are being poured into the moulds which are about 3 feet long. These can tip over causing the molten type metal to pour into the operator's boots. I was present at one such incident and it was awful.

There are a lot of different types of accidents that can happen in the print shop…the most outstanding I ever heard of was when the shop cat, in pursuit of a mouse, took a leap at the mouse and landed on the bed of 4 gang newspress in full speed. It took a week to finally get the press operational again and the type reset for the pages.

Afterword

More history and odds and ends

In the late 70s and early 80s as the ways of typesetting switched more and more to online publishing, more and more small handset type letterpress's became available. The most popular brands in Canada were Pearls and C&P presses usually in the 15 to 20 inch range of size.

Poets and other types of writers took the opportunity to install this equipment in their basements and work sheds. It was a new life for this type of letterpress to flourish. So I was much in demand for a few years installing and training these writers in the craft (which it had now become.

By teaching them how to adjust the make ready which by using various thicknesses of paper and tape underneath the cover sheet which held the various types of pins to hold the paper in registration while it is being inserted into the press. The idea was to make the perfect "kiss" impression on the sheet. Too much pressure could cause too much ink being transferred and causing offset from the sheet to transfer the image to the next page. It was also very hard on the press and the type being used.

I have in my library many examples that these writers/crafts-people produced. Usually bound in boards or cardboard to become books, I am quite fond of them.

This type of production became to be known in Canada and USA as "The Small Press Movement" and championed by Martha Stewart in her Wedding Magazine. Many of the artists used this method to produce very personal types of wedding invitations, menus, etc.

As the growth of these small home based businesses grew there was than a group of people who formed their own small publishing houses to serve the output.

About the Author

You can connect with me on:

🌐 https://artztudio.ca